W9-AHA-999

MISSION TO MARS

THE MARINER MISSIONS TO MARS

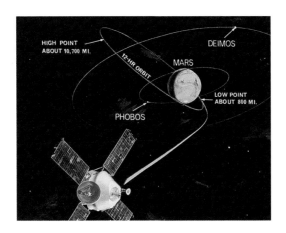

John Hamilton

AB&DO
Daughters Publishing

Visit us at
www.abdopub.com

Published by Abdo Publishing Company, 4940 Viking Drive, Edina, Minnesota 55435.
Copyright ©1998 by Abdo Consulting Group, Inc. International copyrights reserved in all countries. No part of this book may be reproduced in any form without written permission from the publisher.

Interior Graphic Design: John Hamilton
Cover Design: MacLean Tuminelly
Contributing Editor: Alan Gergen

Cover photo: NASA/JPL
Interior photos: NASA/JPL

Sources: Bergamini, David. *The Universe*. New York: Time-Life Books, 1969; Berman, Louis, & Evans, J.C. *Exploring The Cosmos (2nd ed.)*. Boston: Little, Brown and Company, 1977; Caidin, Martin & Barbree, Jay. *Destination Mars*. New York: Penguin Studio, 1997; Campbell, Joseph. *The Power of Myth*. New York: Doubleday, 1988; Crump, Donald, ed. *Frontiers of Science*. Washington, D.C.: National Geographic Society, 1982; Mammana, Dennis. *Mariner*. Microsoft Encarta; *Mariner 4*. Jet Propulsion Laboratory www home page, 1997; *Mariners 6 & 7*. Jet Propulsion Laboratory and NASA's National Space Science Data Center www home page, 1997; Sagen, Carl. *Cosmos*. New York: Random House, 1980; Sheehan, William. *The Planet Mars: A History of Observation and Discovery*. University of Arizona Press, 1996; Weaver, Kenneth. *Mariner 9: Journey to Mars*. National Geographic, February 1973, pp. 231-263; Wilford, John Noble. *Mars Beckons*. New York: Knopf, 1990.

Library of Congress Cataloging–in–Publication Data

Hamilton, John, 1959-
   The Mariner missions to Mars / John Hamilton
      p. cm. — (Mission to Mars)
   Includes index.
   Summary: Describes the Mariner space probe missions carried out between
    1964 and 1972 in order to study the planet Mars.
   ISBN 1-56239-828-8
   1. Project Mariner (U.S.)—Juvenile literature. 2. Space flight to Mars—
Juvenile literature. 3. Mars (Planet)—Exploration—Juvenile literature. 4. Mars
probes—Juvenile literature. [1. Project Mariner (U.S.)] I. Title. II. Series:
Hamilton, John, 1959- Mission to Mars.
TL789.8.U6M34626 1998
629.43' 543—dc21   97-34678
                                       CIP
                                       AC

CONTENTS

CHAPTER 1
THE MARINER MISSIONS

O n November 28, 1964, on a launch pad at NASA's Cape Canaveral in Florida, the worlds of myth and science finally came together. A mighty Atlas-Agena rocket, usually used to launch military missiles, lifted off with a crackling roar, riding a pillar of flame into space. The rocket held an amazing piece of cargo—not a bomb, but the *Mariner 4* spacecraft. Its destination: Mars, fourth planet from the sun.

For thousands of years, people have been in awe of Mars, the Red Planet. They've feared its rusty color, trembled at its strange movements in the night sky, wondering if an alien civilization inhabited its surface, ready to attack an unsuspecting Earth. In Greek and Roman mythology, Mars is the god of war.

Before the *Mariner 4* mission, the only things we knew about Mars we learned through telescopes. These images were blurry at best. But from what astronomers could tell, Mars appeared very similar to Earth. Its diameter is about 4,200 miles (6,758 km), about half that of Earth. Mars is tilted on its axis like Earth, giving it seasons. Also, it rotates on its axis in nearly the same amount of time as Earth, giving it a day that lasts just a little over 24 hours.

Mariner 4 rides into space on an Atlas-Agena rocket.

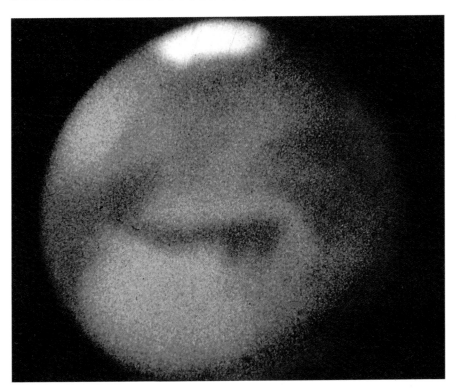

Before the Mariner probes, Mars was very fuzzy when seen by Earth-based telescopes.

It's very cold on Mars, however—the average daytime temperature is only about −22 degrees Fahrenheit (−14 degrees Celsius) at the equator, dropping to −202 degrees Fahrenheit (−130 degrees Celsius) at night.

Polar caps are plainly visible when viewing Mars from a telescope. Astronomers guessed that water was on the planet, perhaps frozen at the poles. But others thought the poles were made of frozen carbon dioxide.

Mars is the only planet that we can see clear surface detail from Earth. (The other planets are too far away, or shrouded in clouds.) In 1877, Italian astronomer Giovanni Schiaparelli announced that he had seen "canali" on the Martian surface. In Italian, "canali" means "channels" or "grooves." People misunderstood Schiaparelli, and thought he meant "canals." They believed that Martians built these canals, and must be part of an advanced civilization.

Schiaparelli and other astronomers also saw large splotches of blue-green color on the mostly reddish Martian surface. The greenish areas seemed to change in size as the seasons came and went. Could they be huge areas of living plants on the Martian surface?

Mariner 4 was launched to help answer some of the many questions swirling around Mars. After nearly eight months of flight through the forbidding vacuum of deep space, *Mariner 4* finally arrived at its destination. What it discovered would stun the scientific community, and change forever the way we look at Mars.

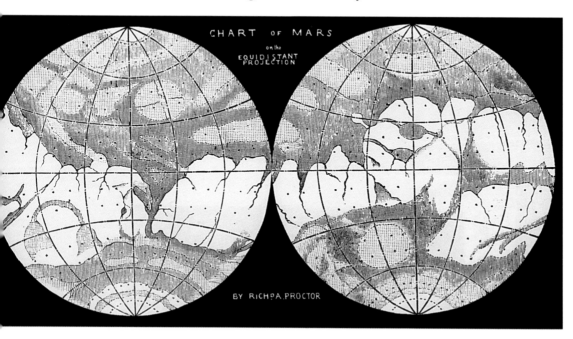

A chart of Mars made by combining the drawings of Schiaparelli and other astronomers.

Chapter 2
. . . .
Mariner 4

Probes are spacecraft that do not have astronauts. Instead, controllers on the ground tell probes what to do. They are first launched into Earth orbit, then sent to their target, where they are told what to photograph or measure. In many cases probes perform their chores automatically, and then send the results back by radio waves to Earth. Sometimes, though, controllers on Earth have to override the probes and perform the experiments manually.

NASA's Mariner program was designed to use interplanetary (between the planets) deep-space probes to explore Earth's nearest neighbors: Mercury, Venus, and Mars. Ten Mariner probes were put into service; seven reached their goals, while three fell short (one failed to launch and two crashed). Of the seven successful missions, four went to Mars.

Russia at this time was competing with America in a "space race." Each country had already sent probes to Venus. Mars was the next prize. The first Russian Mars probe to successfully leave Earth orbit was launched in the fall of 1962, a full two years before *Mariner 4*. But after several months traveling in deep space, radio communications with the probe were suddenly lost. It passed uselessly by the Red Planet, then was lost in space forever.

When *Mariner 4* was ready to launch, scientists at NASA weren't sure what would happen. *Mariner 3* had lifted off earlier that month, but a shroud designed to protect the probe during its flight through Earth's atmosphere failed to eject as planned. NASA soon lost communication with the probe. But when *Mariner 3*'s backup was launched on November 28, everything went smoothly. *Mariner 4* was safely on its way to Mars.

NASA picked a good time to launch *Mariner 4*. November of 1964 was a time when Earth and Mars were near to each other in their orbits. At its closest approach, Mars is 34 million miles (55 million km) from Earth. Launching a spaceship to Mars when the planets are close saves a lot of time and rocket fuel.

Mariner 4 was an amazing piece of equipment for its time, yet it was kept simple in its construction. It was built to withstand the harsh conditions of deep space, including extreme temperatures and radiation. The probe was fitted with four windmill-like solar panels that collected sunlight for electrical power. It had a television camera and six other instruments which scientists hoped to use to measure conditions in space and near Mars. The instrument package included radiometers (to measure the intensity of radiant energy—light or electromagnetic radiation), spectrometers (to measure the wavelength of light), and magnetometers (to measure Mars' magnetic field, if any), and a cosmic dust collector. The total weight of the probe was 575 pounds (261 kg).

Mariner 4's mission was to perform a simple flyby of Mars, instead of going into a complicated insertion orbit.

Seven and a half months after its launch, on July 14, 1965, *Mariner 4* flew over the planet at a distance of about 6,118 miles (9,844 km). As it made its sweep across the rusty-colored Martian landscape, the probe's instruments came to life. *Mariner 4* radioed back to Earth 22 television images, covering about one percent of Mars' surface.

The *Mariner 4* spacecraft, built to withstand the harsh conditions of deep space, used four solar panels to generate electrical power.

The black-and-white images, blurry compared with future probes, nevertheless caused a stir among NASA scientists and astronomers. The surface of Mars wasn't at all what they thought it would be. Instead of vegetation and water, they were greeted with a harsh landscape, a wasteland filled with craters. In fact, Mars looked a lot like Earth's moon.

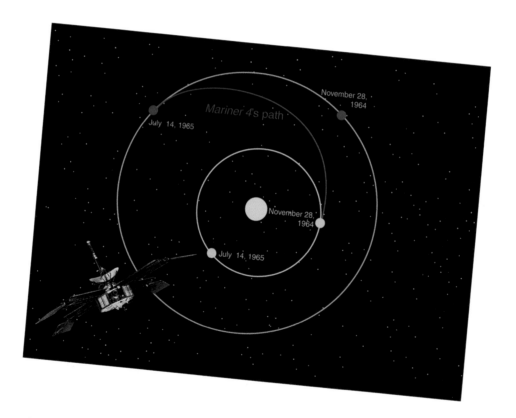

Above: Mariner 4's path through space on its way to the Red Planet.

Facing page: Images sent back from *Mariner 4* showed a heavily cratered Martian surface, much like Earth's moon.

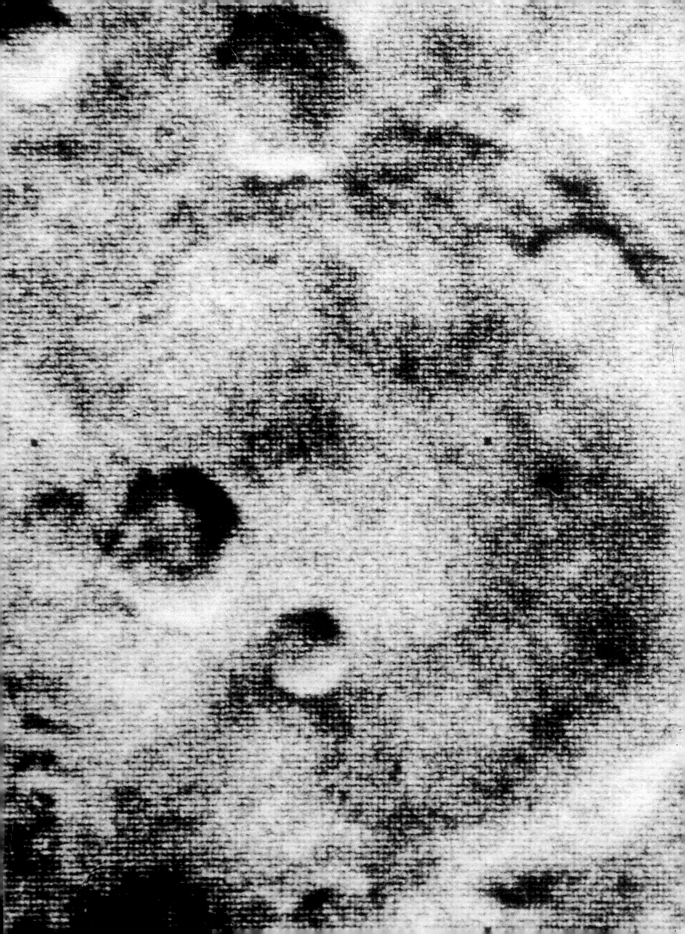

Mariner 4's other instruments detected no magnetic field surrounding Mars, which means it doesn't have a big metallic core like the Earth. The lack of magnetic field meant that scientists didn't have to worry about a dangerous radiation belt around Mars, which would be very hazardous to space probes. But it also meant that cosmic radiation would be about 100 times greater than on Earth, making the planet a dangerous place for future human astronauts.

Mariner 4's instruments gave scientists another surprise: The atmospheric pressure on Mars is only between one and two percent that of Earth. (To find air that thin on Earth, you would have to fly about 20 miles (32 km) above the planet.) What little atmosphere there

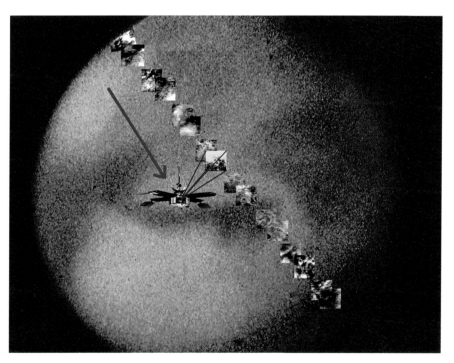

Mariner 4's 22 images covered about one percent of the Martian surface.

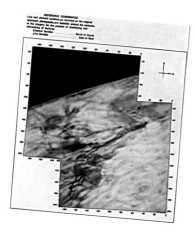

A NASA photo-mosaic combining two of the images sent back from *Mariner 4*.

is on Mars is mostly carbon dioxide. Water in its liquid form could almost certainly not exist on Mars; it would quickly evaporate in the thin Martian air.

Scientists were a little depressed by what *Mariner 4* showed them. There was no vegetation. The changes in colors seen by Earth-based telescopes were almost certainly caused by wind-blown dust storms. And there were no canals on Mars, no advanced civilizations. Schiaparelli's "canali" were probably optical illusions. Mars seemed ancient and dead. But the Red Planet still held a lot of surprises, which astronomers would soon discover.

CHAPTER 3
•••••••••••••
MARINERS 6 AND 7

Mariners 6 and 7 were next in line to travel to the Red Planet. (Earlier, *Mariner 5* went to Venus.) *Mariner 6* blasted off from Cape Canaveral's launch pad 34B on February 24, 1969. *Mariner 7* followed on March 27. Because of the way Earth and Mars aligned, however, the two probes would arrive at Mars only four days apart.

Both spacecraft were redesigned from the earlier *Mariner 4*; the probes were boosted into space by a more powerful Atlas-Centaur rocket, and each craft had an improved array of scientific instruments on board. The new Mariners were bigger and heavier, each weighing about 906 pounds (411 kg). They carried fully automatic instrument packs, including two television cameras, plus infrared and ultraviolet spectrometers.

An Atlas-Centaur rocket, like the one that lifted *Mariners 6, 7,* and *9* toward Mars.

Mariner 6 began the main part of its mission on July 31, 1969, as it flew within 2,175 miles (3,500 km) of Mars. America was already gripped with space fever from the flight of *Apollo 11*, in which Neil Armstrong and Edwin Aldrin became the first astronauts to walk on the moon. Astronomers waited breathlessly for

The redesigned *Mariners 6* and *7* spacecraft had
an improved array of scientific equipment.

Mariner's signals to travel millions of miles back to
Earth. (Russia during this time tried to launch two Mars
probes, but both failed.)

As with *Mariner 4*, *Mariners 6* and *7* were flyby
missions. The probes approached the Red Planet, took
their photographs and measurements, and then slipped
back into deep space. During its flyby, *Mariner 6* recorded
25 close-ups of the Martian surface, mainly of the area

The crater-filled photos sent back by *Mariners 6* and *7* reinforced the idea that Mars had a lunar-like surface.

around the planet's equator. (It also recorded 50 long-distance photos of Mars during the probe's approach.) A few days later *Mariner 7* added 126 photographs of Mars, concentrating on the Southern Hemisphere, including the South Polar Region. In all, the two probes increased our close-up coverage of Mars from *Mariner 4*'s one percent to nearly 10 percent of the planet's surface. The photos the probes sent back were also clearer than *Mariner 4*'s, mainly because of better equipment, and also because the flybys were much closer to the surface.

Mariners 6 and *7* confirmed much of what *Mariner 4* had already revealed. The Martian atmosphere was very thin. There was no trace of a magnetic field. *Mariner 7* recorded the surface temperature of the South Pole at

–190 degrees Fahrenheit (–123 degrees Celsius), which made scientists believe that Mars' polar caps were made of sheets of frozen carbon dioxide.

Mariners 6 and *7* were sent to Mars' Southern Hemisphere on purpose. There was much interest in this area because that's where a lot of the dark areas that were seen from Earth were concentrated. But the photos from the two probes showed even more craters dotting a desert-like surface.

Images returned from *Mariner 7*'s exploration of Mars' south polar cap.

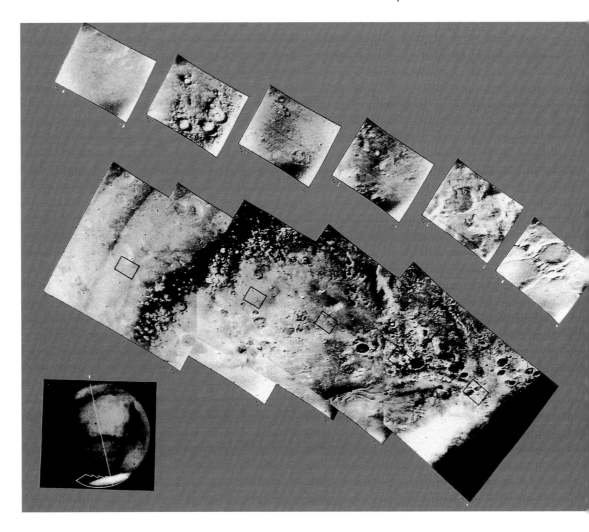

There was one mysterious area, though, that had astronomers puzzled, just when they thought they had Mars figured out. The area is called Heles. It is a large circular basin about 808 miles (1,300 km) across. It is a low-lying area that's surprisingly smooth, with very few craters. If Mars really was a dead planet, with no geological changes for billions of years, then there should have been craters in the Heles region. Astronomers guessed that there must have been some kind of erosion going on down on the Martian surface.

Perhaps Mars wasn't quite so dead after all.

By a twist of fate, the astronomers were looking in the wrong place—the mostly desert Southern Hemisphere. Most of Mars' incredible geological features are in the *Northern* Hemisphere, including enormous volcanoes, canyons, and dry riverbeds. But scientists at that time didn't know this, of course. In the Southern Hemisphere they saw mostly cratered desert terrain—except for the mysterious Heles area. What had caused the erosion?

In order to solve this latest Martian riddle, NASA astronomers needed more than a simple flyby probe— they needed an orbiting satellite. Two years later, they got their wish.

CHAPTER 4

. . . .

Mariner 9

When *Mariner 8* lifted off from Cape Canaveral on May 8, 1971, NASA scientists were excited. A more advanced set of instruments was set to photograph the Martian surface, and this time the probe wouldn't make a quick flyby of the planet; *Mariner 8* was fitted with larger engines to give it the needed boost to put it into orbit around Mars. But the scientists' excitement soon turned to disappointment. Twenty seconds after liftoff, a small electronic part in the rocket's guidance system failed. The second stage of the rocket failed to ignite, and *Mariner 8* crashed into the Atlantic Ocean.

As NASA scrambled to launch a replacement, the Russians launched two probes of their own. *Mars 2* was sent toward the Red Planet on May 19, just 11 days after the failure of *Mariner 8*. *Mars 2* was a huge spacecraft, weighing over five tons (4.5 metric tons). It was an orbiter/lander, designed to send a remote probe to the surface once it reached Mars orbit. A few days later, the Russians launched *Mars 3*, another big orbiter/lander. The race was on.

On May 30, 1971, three days after the Russians launched *Mars 3*, NASA

The *Mariner 9* spacecraft.

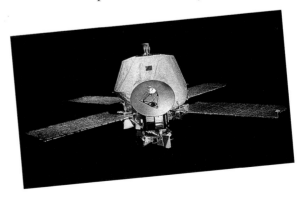

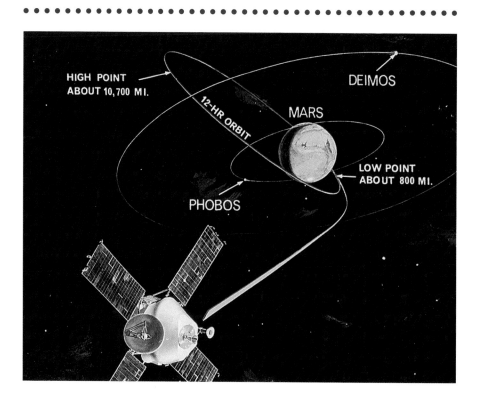

HIGH POINT
ABOUT 10,700 MI.

DEIMOS

MARS

12-HR ORBIT

LOW POINT
ABOUT 800 MI.

PHOBOS

Mariner 9 settled into an elliptical orbit around Mars in November 1971.

sent *Mariner 9* on its way to the Red Planet. This time the liftoff went smoothly. The 1,245-pound (565-kilogram) probe began its journey through 247 million miles (397 million km) of deep space. Five months later, on November 13, 1971, *Mariner 9* slipped into orbit around Mars, beating the two Russian probes.

Mariner 9 was the first spacecraft to orbit another planet. It settled into what is called an "elliptical" orbit, which meant it was close sometimes and then farther away on its journey around the alien world. At its closest approach, *Mariner 9* came to within 868 miles (1,397 km) of the Martian surface, much closer than any of the other Mariner probes.

About two weeks after *Mariner 9* went into orbit around Mars, the two Russian spacecraft arrived. Unfortunately, all three Earth probes were greeted with a disturbing sight: an enormous, planet-wide dust storm was raging on the surface of Mars. The planet was totally hidden from view. Luckily for the Americans, *Mariner 9*'s flight plan was designed to be flexible. NASA engineers shut off the probe's cameras to conserve energy, then parked it in a stable 12-hour orbit to wait out the storm.

The Russians weren't so fortunate. Designed to perform their tasks automatically, the probes dropped their landers into the storms raging below. The descent module from *Mars 2* failed completely and crashed. But in doing so, it became the first human object to reach Mars. The Russians even put a pennant with the insignia of the Soviet Union inside the lander so future Mars explorers would know where it came from.

Mars 3 had more luck. The lander actually touched down safely on the surface with the help of parachutes and rockets. It sent back a television image for a few seconds, and then suddenly contact was lost forever. Some scientists guessed that the lander was blown over by the Martian storm. We may never know *Mars 3*'s final fate.

The Russian orbiters didn't do too well either. They dutifully sent back photo after photo of cloud-covered Mars. Although other instruments did send back some useful information, for the most part *Mars 3* and *Mars 4* were disappointing failures.

Mariner 9, meanwhile, patiently waited for the dust storm to clear. A month later, the winds died down, and NASA scientists switched the probe's cameras back on. The images *Mariner 9* finally sent back to Earth were astonishing—Mars turned out to be a very interesting place indeed.

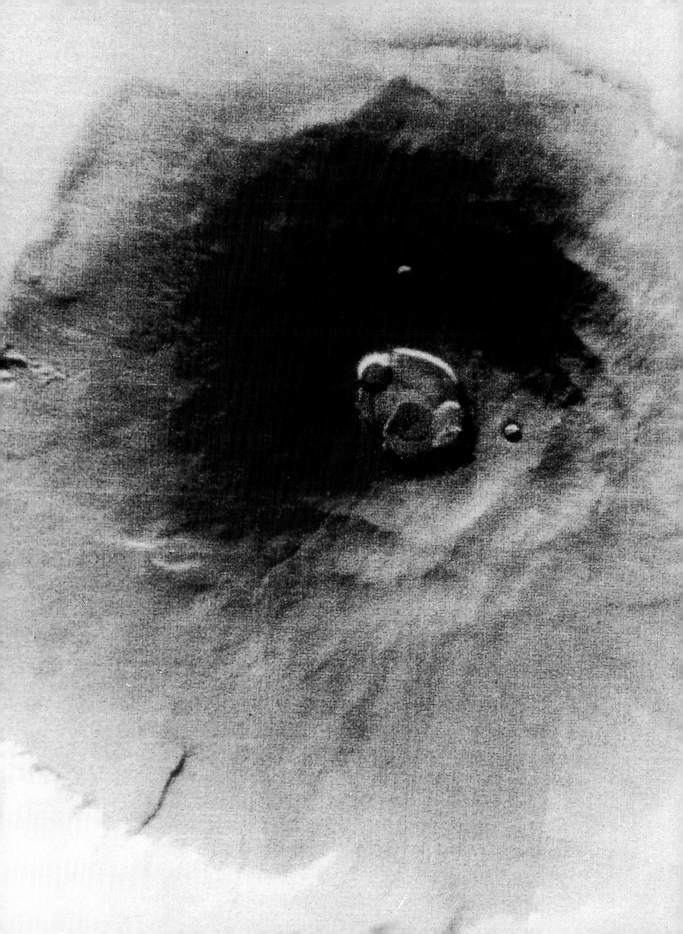

CHAPTER 5
VOLCANOES, CANYONS, AND MOONS

For nearly a full year, *Mariner 9* returned 7,329 images of Mars, mapping 100 percent of the surface. When the probe relayed photos from the planet's Northern Hemisphere, NASA scientists were staggered at the dramatic landscapes *Mariner 9* revealed.

When Mars was covered by the great dust storm of 1971, there was a series of large dark spots dotting the Tharsis region that astronomers couldn't explain. When the dust storm cleared and *Mariner 9* began its mapping mission, these spots were the first features to be revealed. They turned out to be a series of enormous shield volcanoes. The largest was Nix Olympica, which was later renamed Olympus Mons. This giant volcano dwarfs anything found on Earth. In fact, it's the tallest mountain in the whole solar system. It is almost 373 miles (600 km) wide at its base, as large as the state of Arizona. Olympus Mons rises nearly 16 miles (25 km) above the surrounding

Facing page: Olympus Mons, the tallest known mountain in the entire solar system.

Martian plains, over twice as high as Earth's Mount Everest. The super volcano's central crater, or caldera, is a complex, multi-volcanic vent that is nearly 50 miles (80 km) across. In addition to Olympus Mons, *Mariner 9* revealed three other giant volcanoes: Ascraeus Mons, Pavonis Mons, and Arsia Mons.

Mariner 9 photographed another amazing discovery, a spectacular canyon stretching across almost one fourth of Mars' surface. Named Vallis Marineris (in honor of the Mariner missions), this giant rift in the Martian landscape cuts across the equatorial region. Like the Great Rift Valley of Africa, it was probably formed by massive shifting of the planet's crust. Vallis Marineris is nearly 3,000 miles (4,827 km) long and up to 15.5 miles (25 km) wide. In some places the canyon is almost four and one-half miles (seven km) deep. Vallis Marineris makes Earth's Grand Canyon (about 1 mile (1.6 km) deep and 200 miles (321 km) long) look like a gully!

A section of Vallis Marineris, the 3,000-mile (4,827-km) long canyon that stretches across Mars.

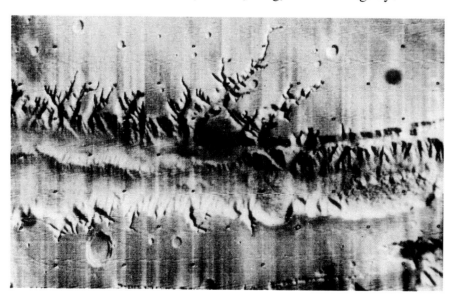

In addition to mapping the Red Planet's surface details, *Mariner 9* set another record—the probe took the first close-up photos of Mars' two tiny moons, Phobos and 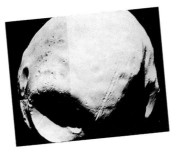 Phobos, one of Mars' two moons. *(Image taken by the Viking orbiter in 1976.)* Deimos. Phobos is a potato-shaped chunk of crater-marked rock, only about 14 miles (22.5 km) in diameter. Deimos is similar in shape, but about half as large. Both are probably asteroids, captured by Mars' gravity shortly after the planet was formed.

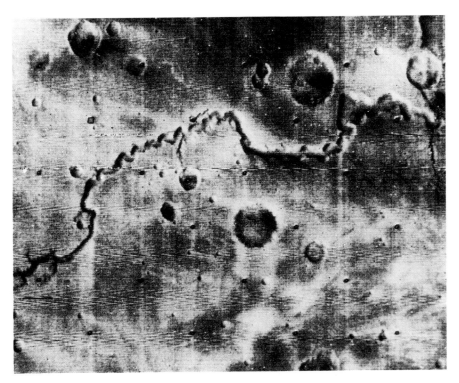

A photo mosaic of Vallis Marineris from a height of 18,645 miles (30,000 kilometers).

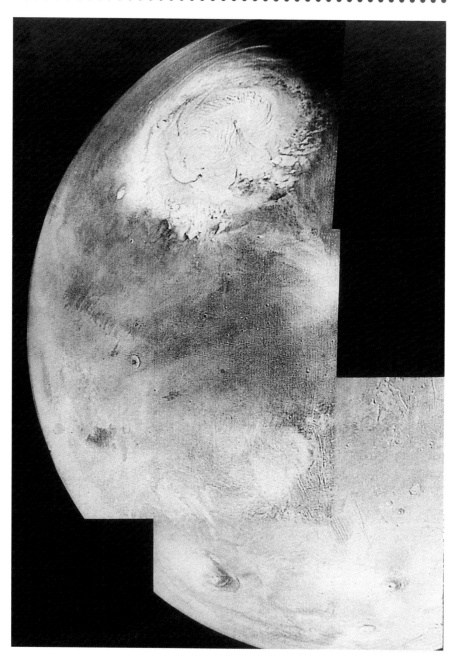

Mars' north polar ice cap. Scientists wondered: could there be frozen water hidden beneath the thick layer of frozen carbon dioxide?

CHAPTER 6
WATER AND...
LIFE?

Perhaps the finding that caused the most excitement among astronomers was the discovery of ancient, dry riverbeds on the planet's surface. These are carved into what at first seemed to be a dry, dusty, lifeless planet. Scientists were astonished; there must have been running water on Mars long ago! This was probably the biggest discovery of *Mariner 9*, because it meant that at one time, perhaps Mars wasn't the hostile place that we see today. Maybe long ago life flourished on its surface, as it does today on Earth. Maybe, just maybe, there's still life clinging to that remote, forbidding planet.

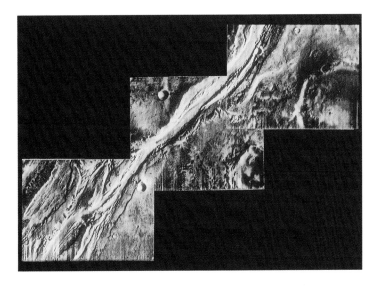

An ancient riverbed cutting across the Martian surface.

Despite the harsh conditions on Mars—the below-zero temperatures, the thin, bone-dry atmosphere, the high levels of radiation from the sun—it seemed possible that some kind of alien life might exist there. Most scientists thought that if they discovered life on Mars, it would be primitive—bacteria, perhaps; moss or lichens at best. Nothing that the Mariner missions had discovered ruled out *some* kind of life, however. It was a remote chance, but still a chance nevertheless.

But if we wanted to find out for sure if something was still alive on the Red Planet, we had to do better than observe from orbit; we had to get down to the surface. The only way to tell for sure was to send a lander. The search for possible life on Mars gave a big push for the next series of probes that would arrive in the mid-1970s—the Viking missions.

An artist's conception of a Viking lander touching down on the surface of Mars.

INTERNET SITES

Starchild: A learning center for young astronomers
http://starchild.gsfc.nasa.gov/

This lively site, a service of the Laboratory for High Energy Astrophysics at NASA, is full of information on the solar system, astronauts, and space travel. It has a very good section on Mars covering the main features of the red planet, including photos.

Mars Missions
http://mpfwww.jpl.nasa.gov/

This NASA web page provides up-to-the-minute information and photographs on three current space probes: *Mars Pathfinder*, *Mars Global Surveyor*, and *Mars Surveyor 98*.

The Whole Mars Catalog
http://www.reston.com/astro/mars/catalog.html

This is a very extensive site of Mars facts and photos, with many links to other related web sites. Some of the many topics include Mars facts, breaking news from NASA, space probes, and the push to put humans on Mars.

These sites are subject to change. Go to your favorite search engine and type in "Mars" for more sites.

PASS IT ON

Space buffs: educate readers around the country by passing on information you've learned about Mars and space exploration. Share your little-known facts and interesting stories. We want to hear from you!

To get posted on the ABDO & Daughters website, E-mail us at "Science@abdopub.com"

Visit the ABDO & Daughters website at www.abdopub.com

GLOSSARY

· · · · · · · · · · · · · · · · · · ·

mythology

A collection of stories and folk tales that explain the history of a civilization and its peoples, including their gods, ancestors, and heroes.

probe

A probe is an unmanned space vehicle that is sent on missions that are too dangerous, or would take too long, for human astronauts to accomplish. Probes are equipped with many scientific instruments, like cameras and radiation detectors. Information from these instruments is radioed back to ground controllers on Earth.

rocket

A vehicle that moves because of the ejection of gases made by the burning of a self-contained propellant. The propellant is made up of fuel, like liquid hydrogen, and an oxidant like liquid oxygen, which helps the fuel to burn. Sometimes solid explosives are used, like nitroglycerin and nitrocellulose. Solid-fuel rockets are more reliable, but generate less thrust. Some spacecraft, like the United States' Space Shuttle, use a combination of solid and liquid fuel rocket boosters. Rockets were probably invented by the Chinese almost 1,000 years ago, when they stuffed gunpowder into bamboo pipes to make weapons.

solar panel

Many space probes use solar panels, which are large arrays of connected solar cells, to generate electricity. Solar cells are semiconductor devices that convert the energy of sunlight into electric energy. Electricity is needed to power the probe's science experiments, guidance systems, and radios. Some probes, especially those that travel far from the sun to explore the outer planets, rely on internal nuclear power plants to generate electricity. The *Cassini* probe to Saturn, launched in October of 1997 and due to arrive in 2004, uses a nuclear generator.

solar system

The sun, the nine planets, and other celestial bodies (like asteroids) that orbit the sun. The nine planets are (in order from the sun): Mercury, Venus, Earth, Mars, Jupiter, Saturn, Uranus, Neptune, and Pluto.

star

A large, self-containing ball of gas that is "self luminous," or emits light. Stars come in many sizes, ranging from white dwarfs to red giants. The sun is a medium-sized yellow star. At night, stars are seen as twinkling points of light, which is one way to tell them apart from planets, which do not twinkle.

telescope

A device to detect and observe distant objects by their reflection or emission of various kinds of electromagnetic radiation (like light). Most astronomy research today is conducted with telescopes that detect electromagnetic radiation other than visible light, such as radio or x-ray telescopes.

INDEX